Savvy

Fit Girl

Yoga for FITNESS AND FLEXIBILITY

by Rebecca Rissman

CAPSTONE PRESS
a capstone imprint

Savvy Books are published by Capstone Press.
1710 Roe Crest Drive, North Mankato, Minnesota 56003
www.capstonepub.com

Library of Congress Cataloging-in-Publication Data

Cataloging-in-Publication Data in on file with the Library of Congress.

ISBN 978-1-4914-2120-8 (library binding)
ISBN 978-1-4914-2361-5 (eBook PDF)

Editorial Credits
Mandy Robbins, editor; Heidi Thompson, designer; Sarah Schuette, prop preparation; Marcy Morin, scheduler; Charmaine Whitman, production specialist

Photo Credits
Capstone Studio: TJ Thoraldson Digital Photography, all photos except; iStockphoto, Inc: arekmalang, 60, mandygodbehear, 18 (top), sparks_chen, 5; Shutterstock: B Calkins, 7, Ikoimages, 6, Syda Productions, 18 (bottom), takayuki, 58

Design Elements
Shutterstock: A-R-T, redstone, vectorkat

Printed in Canada.
092014   008478FRS15

TABLE OF *Contents*

GET Fit
with *Yoga!*

You're no couch potato. But you get tired of doing the same old workout routine. You can only jog around the block so many times before boredom creeps in. It's time to mix things up, and yoga might just be the answer.

Go ahead—flex your muscles. Want to see more definition? One of the biggest perks of a regular yoga practice is that it builds muscle. Practice yoga regularly and you'll see muscles you didn't even know you had! Not only does yoga help you grow stronger, but it also helps you become more flexible. This is an important counterpart to having muscular strength. After all, what good are toned hamstrings if you can't reach down to tie your shoes?

Yoga is a combination of three things: physical poses called *asanas*, controlled breathing called *pranayama*, and meditation. When used together, this combo benefits people of all ages. In fact, people who practice yoga often report that they sleep better, get sick less often, feel happier, and are less overwhelmed by worries.

Stay Safe

Yoga is only beneficial if you remember one very important rule—never do anything in yoga that causes you pain. When performed correctly, a yoga pose might make you feel a muscular challenge or deep stretch. It should never, ever cause pain. Follow this rule in all types of yoga poses.

Pronounced: prah-nah-YAH-mah

From the root *prana* meaning breath, or life force

Pranayama is the practice of controlling the breath. It often involves retaining, or holding the breath for a few seconds at a time in a careful rhythm directed by an instructor.

Is Yoga Just for Flexible People?

When was the last time you touched your toes? If it's been a while, don't worry. One myth about yoga is that only flexible people can do it. But practicing yoga on a regular basis is actually one of the best ways to *become* flexible. Yoga poses can be modified for any yoga student, regardless of how flexible he or she is.

Vinyasa Yoga is one type of yoga that can help people become more flexible. This type of yoga involves flowing from pose to pose. There is less rest between poses, which can make this type of yoga physically challenging.

Yoga Strap

A yoga strap is a simple but useful yoga prop. Yoga straps can be used to help modify poses. They can help you extend your reach if you're not quite flexible enough to perform the full version of a pose. For example, if you're not able to touch your toes in a forward fold, hook the strap across the balls of your feet and enjoy the stretch.

SUN SALUTATION A

Sanskrit Name: Surya Namaskar A

Pronounced: SIR-yah NAH-ma-skar

Almost all yoga classes will include Sun Salutations. Sun Salutations are a sequence of poses designed to energize the body, warm the muscles, and help people get focused on their body. Sun Salutations involve large gentle movements. They increase blood flow to all the muscle groups of the body. In a typical yoga practice, you will do at least three Sun Salutations at the start of class. Then, you might continue to do Sun Salutations between poses to raise your heart rate or keep your muscles warm.

Sun Salutations have ancient roots. The name *namaskar* comes from the word *nama*, which means to "bow down" or "adore." When early yoga students practiced Sun Salutations, they were bowing down to the sun. Today people still value the symbolism of this activity. It's a reminder of the importance of the sun to the living things that need it.

MOUNTAIN POSE

Sanskrit Name: Tadasana

Pronounced: tah-DAH-sah-nah

step 1 Mountain Pose starts out each Sun Salutation. To begin, stand at the top of your mat with your big toes touching and your heels slightly separated.

step 2 Spread your toes out on the mat.

step 3 Stand up tall. Roll your shoulders down your back. Bring your shoulder blades closer together and pull them down.

step 4 Let your arms hang at your sides. Face your palms forward.

step 5 Lift your chin slightly so that your jawbone is parallel to the floor.

Drop your shoulders and lengthen your neck.

Face your palms forward.

FORWARD FOLD

Sanskrit Name: *Uttanasana*

Pronounced: ooh-tah-NAH-sah-nah

After Mountain Pose, the Sun Salutation moves into a Forward Fold. This might seem like a simple movement, but it's actually a challenge to focus on finding the right alignment. Paying attention to the position of your feet, back, knees, and gaze will make this seemingly easy pose very challenging.

step 1 Start in Mountain Pose. Inhale and lift your arms up.

step 2 With a slight bend in your knees, exhale and bend at the hips to fold forward.

step 3 Allow your hands to rest on your shins, ankles, the floor, or on blocks.

step 4 If this feels challenging, keep your knees slightly bent. If you want more of a stretch, slowly straighten your knees.

HALF-FORWARD FOLD

Sanskrit Name: *Arda Uttanasana*

Pronounced: ARE-duh ooh-tah-NAH-sah-nah

step 1 From Forward Fold, you will move into the next pose in the Sun Salutation. Inhale and lift your head and shoulders away from the floor.

step 2 With straight elbows, rest your hands on the floor, blocks, your ankles, or your shins.

step 3 Extend the crown of your head forward, so that your back becomes straight.

step 4 Focus your gaze on the mat.

step 5 Return to your full Forward Fold as you exhale.

FOUR-LIMBED STAFF POSE

Sanskrit Name: *Chaturanga Dandasana*

Pronounced: chah-turr-AN-gah don-DAHS-ah-nah

After your Forward Fold, you will move into Four-Limbed Staff Pose. This pose takes a bit of practice to get down. Asking a friend to watch you move through this pose can be very helpful. She can let you know if you need to adjust your alignment.

step 1 From your Forward Fold, bend your knees enough to bring both palms flat on your yoga mat just outside of your feet. Your hands should be about shoulder-distance apart on the mat.

step 2 Step back into Plank Pose. This pose looks like you are about to do a pushup. Have your feet about 2 to 3 inches (5 to 8 cm) apart, and rest your weight on the balls of your feet. Make sure your shoulders are right above your wrists.

Plank Pose

step 3 Straighten your back as much as possible. A good way to do this is to point your tailbone toward your heels. At the same time, point the crown of your head forward.

step 4 Bend your elbows to lower your body halfway down to the mat. Stop when your elbows are at the same height as your shoulders. Make sure to keep your elbows tucked in close to your ribcage. Do not let them bend out to the sides the way you might in a typical pushup.

→ If this feels too challenging or hurts your back in any way, modify this pose by bringing your knees to the mat. It is better to modify a move and keep proper form than to push your body to do things it's not ready for.

Keep your body parallel to the floor.

Four-Limbed Staff Pose is typically followed by one of two back-bending poses: Cobra Pose or Upward Facing Dog Pose. Cobra is a gentler pose. If you tweaked your back carrying too many books, this is the pose for you. If you're looking for more of a challenge to your core, shoulders, and legs, give Upward Facing Dog a try.

COBRA POSE

Sanskrit Name: *Bhujangasana*
Pronounced: boo-john-GAHS-ah-nah

step 1 From Four-Limbed Staff Pose, lower your stomach down to your mat.

step 2 Point your toes and press the tops of your feet into the mat.

step 3 Roll your shoulders up and back. Then press into your hands to lift your head and shoulders away from the mat. Lift your chin slightly.

step 4 Keep your elbows slightly bent and pinned to your sides. Try to use the muscles in your back and the muscles in your arms to hold this gentle backbend.

UPWARD FACING DOG

Urdhva Mukha Svanasana

Sanskrit Name: **Urdhva Mukha Svanasana**

Pronounced: OORD-vah MOOK-ah svan-AHS-ah-nah

step 1 From Four-Limbed Staff Pose you could move right into Upward Facing Dog instead of Cobra pose. Just press your weight into the tops of the feet and lift the rest of your body up. Keep your knees straight.

step 2 Straighten your elbows to lift your shoulders away from the floor. At the same time, drop your hips to come into a backbend. Keep your knees and hips off the mat.

step 3 Pull your shoulders down away from your ears and lift your chin slightly.

DOWNWARD FACING DOG

Sanskrit Name: *Adho Mukha Svanasana*

Pronounced: AH-doh MOOK-ah svan-AHS-ah-nah

You'll finish your Sun Salutation in yoga's most famous pose—Downward Facing Dog. In many yoga classes, you will do this pose over and over again. Because it is such a staple of most yoga practices, it's important to do it correctly.

step 1 From Cobra Pose or Upward Facing Dog Pose, tuck your toes under and use the muscles of your core to lift your bottom up. Your body will form the shape of an upside-down V.

step 2 Press your heels toward the mat. If you are able, straighten your knees. If this feels too intense, allow your knees to stay bent.

Press down through all parts of your palms.

step 3 Press all parts of your hands evenly down into the mat, especially the area around your thumb and the base of each finger. Don't let all of your weight rest on your wrists. This can lead to painful joint problems.

step 4 Pull your belly in toward your spine.

Try to think about your Sun Salutations as a way to rev up your yoga practice. Add a Sun Salutation in at any point during your yoga practice. Doing this will energize your body and refocus your mind.

Pull your belly button in toward your spine.

Press your heels down toward the mat.

Using YOGA to Gain
FLEX-IBILITY

After a few Sun Salutations, you're probably feeling the burn. The time is right to work on poses that build flexibility. Yoga is a safe way to become more flexible because it lengthens your muscles without overstretching or injuring them. Yoga requires you to keep your muscles active as you stretch. When muscles are completely relaxed, they can be easily injured.

Don't hurry to become more flexible. A regular yoga practice will help you to gradually build flexibility over time. It can be tempting to try to push yourself to achieve different challenging poses you see other people doing. But it's much safer to pace yourself. Slow and steady is the way to go.

Don't lock your joints while practicing yoga. Always keep a very slight bend in joints such as your knees and elbows. Doing this will keep your muscles active. It will also prevent you from overstretching.

WARRIOR 1 POSE

Sanskrit Name: *Virabhadrasana*

Pronounced: vee-rah-bah-DRAS-ah-nah

It might seem odd to hear a yoga pose called "warrior." After all, we often think of yoga as a peaceful activity. This pose is named in honor of a special type of warrior—the spiritual warrior. Traditionally, the people who practiced yoga in ancient India were fighting to learn more about themselves. Because of this, they are sometimes called warriors of the spirit.

step 1 From Downward Facing Dog, step your left foot forward between your hands.

step 2 Turn your right heel down to the mat. The inner edge of your right foot should press down into the mat. Keep your right leg straight.

step 3 Inhale and lift your upper body and arms up. Straighten your elbows and face your palms toward one another. Relax your shoulders down away from your ears.

step 4 Exhale and bend deeply into your left knee until it hovers over your left ankle.

step 5 Lift your chin and look up between your hands. Hold for a few breaths.

step 6 Return to Downward Facing Dog Pose. Repeat on the other side.

Press your heel into the mat.

21

HALF-SPLITS POSE

Sanskrit Name: *Ardha Hanumanasana*

Pronounced: ARE-duh hah-noo-mah-NAHS-ah-nah

Half-Splits Pose is also sometimes called Half-Monkey God pose. This name comes from a story about Hanuman, a god from the Hindu religion. In the story, Hanuman leaps across an ocean with one leg stretched out in front of him and one stretched behind him. When people do the full version of the pose, they resemble Hanuman as he leapt.

step 1 From Downward Facing Dog, step your right foot forward between your hands. Bend your right knee deeply.

step 2 Bring your left knee down to the mat. Keep your left toes tucked under and your left heel lifted.

step 3 Bring your hands to either side of your right knee on the mat.

step 4 Slowly, start to straighten your right knee by moving your hips backward. Stop when the stretch feels challenging but not painful.

step 5 Try to hover your hips above your left knee. If you need to, move your left knee back on the mat a few inches.

step 6 Flex your right foot so that your toes point straight up.

step 7 Fold your head and chest forward.

! The full version of this pose is very challenging. Work with a yoga instructor to make sure you have the correct alignment.

Splits Pose

Tuck your toes under.

WIDE-LEGGED FORWARD FOLD

Sanskrit Name: *Prasarita Padottanasana*

Pronounced: prah-sah-REE-tah pah-doh-tah-NAHS-ah-nah

The Wide-Legged Forward Fold provides a challenging stretch in what looks like an easy pose. But if your muscles are engaged and properly aligned, your back, thighs, and feet will all be working hard.

step 1 Start in Mountain Pose.

step 2 Take a big step out to the right so that your feet are at least 3 feet (1 meter) apart. Have your toes slightly closer together than your heels.

step 3 Bring your hands to your hips.

step 4 Put a slight bend in your knees and bend at the hips to fold forward.

step 5 Bring your hands down to the mat directly under your shoulders.

step 6 As you inhale, straighten your elbows and lift your upper body halfway away from the floor.

Mountain Pose

step 7 As you exhale, bend your elbows and fold forward. Keep the muscles in your back active by pulling your shoulder blades toward your hips.

step 8 Press evenly into the inner and outer edges of your feet.

step 9 If you are able, slowly begin to straighten your knees but stop before you lock them.

25

COW-FACE POSE

Sanskrit Name: *Gomukhasana*

Pronounced: go-moo-KAHS-ah-nah

If you look closely at Cow-Face Pose you might be able to see how it resembles a cow's face. The crossed legs look like a cow's crooked jaw. The elbows look like a cow's floppy ears. This oddly named pose works your back and core while stretching your hips and shoulders.

step 1 Start on your hands and knees. Cross your left knee behind your right. Allow your feet to fall out to the sides.

step 2 Slowly, walk your hands back as you sit your bottom down between your heels. If this feels like too much of a stretch on your knees, place a block between your ankles and sit on that.

step 3 Bring your upper body upright to sit up tall.

step 4 Lift your left arm straight up. Bend the left elbow to reach your hand toward your middle back.

step 5 Reach your right arm straight out to the right with your palm facing behind you. Bend your right elbow to bring the back of your right hand toward the middle of your back.

step 6 If you are able, clasp your hands behind your back. If this is too challenging, either hold a yoga strap or towel between your hands, or simply grab hold of your shirt with each hand.

step 7 Lift your chin slightly and sit up straight. Hold for a few breaths.

step 8 Repeat on the other side.

27

COBBLER'S POSE

Sanskrit Name: *Baddha Konasana*

Pronounced: BAH-dah kone-AHS-ah-nah

Do you need an excuse to inspect your pedicure? Cobbler's Pose will give you that chance. Cobblers are people who repair shoes. Cobbler's Pose looks like someone examining the soles of her shoes. This pose stretches your hips, low back, and neck.

step 1 Start sitting on your mat. Bring the soles of your feet together, and let your knees fall open to the sides.

step 2 Slide your feet closer to your body until you begin to feel a stretch in your hips. This will be a different distance for everyone. Some people might be able to bring their heels all the way to the body, while others might have to stop when their heels are 12 or 18 inches (30 or 45 cm) away. Either way is okay.

step 3 Sit up tall. Pull your shoulders down away from your ears.

step 4 Bring your thumbs to the balls of your feet and pull the big-toe sides of your feet open. It will look a little like you are opening a book.

step 5 Keep your hips relaxed. Pull your belly button in toward your spine. Hold for a few breaths.

Alignment matters in this pose. If your knees begin to rise up higher than your hips, sit on top of a yoga block. This way you can keep your knees at the same height as your hips.

ONE-LEGGED KING PIGEON POSE

Sanskrit Name: *Eka Pada Rajakapotasana*

Pronounced: EH-kah PAH-dah rah-jah-cop-poh-TAHS-ah-nah

If you thought Cow-Face Pose was an odd name, One-Legged King Pigeon Pose may seem even stranger. Whether you say the English or Sanskrit name for this pose, your tongue is going to get as much of a workout as the rest of your body. One-Legged King Pigeon Pose stretches the hips, an area of the body that most people find very tight.

step 1   Start in Downward Facing Dog Pose. Lift your left foot away from the mat.

step 2   Bring your left foot forward to rest on the mat behind your right hand. At the same time, rest your left knee behind your left hand. The outside of your left shin will rest against the floor. If you are very flexible, your left shin might be parallel to the top of your mat. However, for most people, it will be on an angle.

Downward Facing Dog

Point your toes.

step 3 Point your right toes. Allow your right knee to rest on the mat.

step 4 Let your hips fall toward the mat. If this feels painful, place a block or blanket under the left side of your bottom and rest your weight on it. Otherwise, allow your bottom to rest on the mat.

step 5 Keep your upper body upright. Look straight ahead.

step 6 Hold for a few breaths. Carefully return to Downward Facing Dog.

step 7 Repeat on the other side.

ONE-LEGGED KING PIGEON POSE
variation

Once you've mastered One-Legged King Pigeon Pose, you can start working on the many variations commonly practiced in yoga. This pose can be modified in many ways, but one of the most popular ways the pose is performed includes a deep thigh stretch.

King Pigeon Pose with Thigh Stretch

step 1 Start in One-Legged King Pigeon Pose with the right leg forward.

step 2 If your right shin is parallel or close to parallel to the top of the mat, inch your right ankle closer to your groin.

step 3 Keeping your hands directly under your shoulders, bend your elbows to lean your upper body slightly forward.

step 4 Bend your left knee to bring your left ankle in toward your bottom.

step 5 Keep your right hand on the mat while you reach back with your left hand for the outer edge of your left ankle. If you aren't able to grasp the ankle with your hand, try using a yoga strap or towel to extend your reach.

step 6 Square your hips. To do this, point your hips and belly button toward the front of the room or yoga mat.

step 7 Hold for a few breaths. Release into One-Legged King Pigeon Pose, then move to Downward Facing Dog Pose.

step 8 Repeat on the other side.

Downward Facing Dog

33

STANDING PIGEON POSE

If you'd like to focus on balance in addition to stretching, try Standing Pigeon Pose. It offers a deep stretch without putting as much pressure on your hips as One-Legged King Pigeon. Don't be fooled, though—this variation isn't necessarily easier.

step 1 Start in Mountain Pose.

step 2 Bend both knees deeply, as if you were about to sit into a chair.

step 3 Keeping your left knee bent, bring your right ankle on top of the left knee.

step 4 Bring your palms together in front of your heart.

step 5 Bend your left knee more deeply to sit even lower. Keep your right foot flexed.

step 6 Relax your shoulders. Pull your belly button in toward your spine, and keep your upper body tall. Focus your gaze on something directly in front of you.

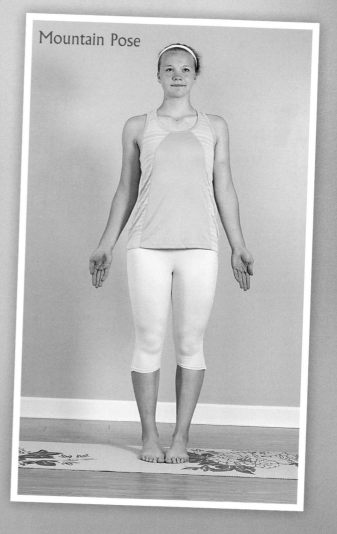

Mountain Pose

Press your hands together over your heart.

step 7 Hold for a few breaths. Slowly return to Mountain Pose.

step 8 Repeat on the other side.

Flex your foot.

UPWARD-FACING BOW POSE

Sanskrit Name: *Urdhva Dhanurasana*

Pronounced: OOR-dva don-your-AHS-ah-nah

Do you ever feel like you're bending over backward to get everything done in your busy schedule? Upward-Facing Bow Pose will teach you to do just that—literally! This pose is an intense, invigorating backbend. With careful practice almost anyone can enjoy this pose.

step 1 Lie on your back on your yoga mat.

step 2 Bend your knees up, and set your feet on the mat a few inches in front of your bottom. Have your feet no wider than the width of your hips.

step 3 Bring your hands with the palms down onto the mat beside your ears with your thumbs pointing toward your cheeks. Have your hands about shoulder-distance apart on the mat. If you have them too close together, this pose can be difficult. Your elbows should rise straight up. Do not allow them to fall out to the sides.

step 3

step 4 As you inhale, press your feet down to lift your hips off the mat. Press into the inner edges of both feet to keep your knees from falling out to the sides.

step 5 As you exhale, press into your hands to lift your head off the mat. Look to the back of your mat to bring the crown of your head down onto the mat.

step 6 Gently pause on the crown of your head without putting pressure on your neck. Bring your elbows slightly closer together, and pull your shoulder blades closer together on your back.

step 7 Pause for a few breaths on the crown of your head. Keep pressing down into the mat with your hands so that you aren't supporting much weight with your head.

step 8 If this feels like a good challenge, stay here. Hold this pose for a few breaths. Then slowly lower to your back for a rest. If you'd like to push yourself even more, turn the page.

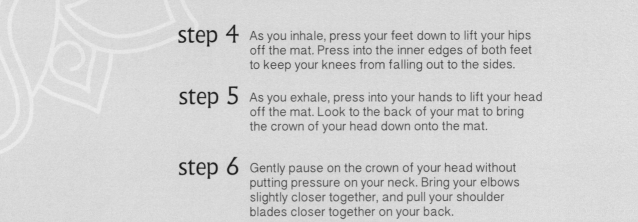

continue on page 38 ➞

UPWARD-FACING BOW POSE
continued

step 9 If you want to try the full Upward-Facing Bow Pose, press into your hands and straighten your elbows to lift your head off the mat.

step 10 Try your best to bring your shoulders directly over your wrists.

step 11 Keep pressing into the inner edges of your feet as you lift your hips higher to bring your knees directly over your ankles. Hold for a few breaths.

step 12 To come out of this pose, tuck your chin into your chest.

step 13 Slowly bend your elbows to return to your back.

step 14 Remain on your back for a few breaths to rest.

step 15 One leg at a time, straighten your knees to lie flat on your mat.

It can be helpful to ask a friend to watch you do this pose to check your alignment.

PYRAMID POSE

Sanskrit Name: *Parsvottanasana*

Pronounced: pars-voh-toe-NAS-ah-nah

Pyramid Pose combines a deep forward fold with an intense hip and thigh stretch. It is also a challenge to balance. Try to think about your alignment as much as possible in this pose. It's better to be in proper alignment and not stretch as deeply. If you force yourself into the full stretch without the right alignment, you could risk injury.

step 1 Start in Downward Facing Dog Pose.

Downward Facing Dog

Straighten your front leg as much as is comfortable.

step 2 Step both feet forward about 12 inches (30 cm).

step 3 Look forward, and step your right foot up between your hands.

step 4 Turn your left heel down and press the inner edge of your left foot down into the mat. Keep your left leg straight.

step 5 Bring your fingertips to the mat on either side of your right foot or allow them to rest on blocks.

step 6 Slowly begin to straighten your right knee. Stop before the stretch becomes painful.

step 7 Allow your upper body to fold forward over your right leg.

step 8 Square your hips. Hold for several breaths.

step 9 Return to Downward Facing Dog Pose. Repeat on the other side.

Keep your back leg straight.

BIG TOE POSE

Sanskrit Name: *Padangusthasana*

Pronounced: pah-dahn-goose-TAHS-ah-nah

You probably never thought something called Big Toe Pose could provide a deep stretch for the shoulders and neck. But think again! Big Toe Pose uses a simple bind to incorporate the upper body in an easy way. Binds can make a pose more intense.

 step 1 Start in Mountain Pose. Reach your arms up.

step 2 With a slight bend in your knees, bend at the hips to fold forward. Allow your hands to fall down toward the mat.

step 3 Bend your knees as much as you need to in order to reach your toes. Hold on to your big toes with your first two fingers. Do not rest your thumbs on the mat.

step 4 As you inhale, slightly lift your head and chest away from the floor. Straighten your elbows and lengthen your back as much as possible. Do not let go of your toes.

step 5 Exhale and fold forward. If you can, start to straighten your knees very slowly.

Mountain Pose

step 6 If you are able to straighten your knees, bend your elbows out to the sides. Pull your upper body closer to your thighs.

step 7 Hold for a few breaths. Return to Mountain Pose.

43

LOW-LUNGE POSE

Sanskrit Name: *Anjanayasana*

Pronounced: on-jen-eh-AHS-ah-nah

It's time to get low! Low-Lunge Pose stretches your hips, thighs, and ankles while strengthening your upper back and arms.

step 1 From Downward Facing Dog Pose, step your right foot forward between your hands.

step 2 Drop your left knee to the mat, and point your left toes.

step 3 Bring both hands to the top of your right knee.

step 4 Slowly begin to move your hips forward until you feel a deep stretch in the front of your left hip and right buttock.

step 5 Inhale and lift your arms up with your palms facing one another. Straighten your elbows.

Keep your toes flat on the floor

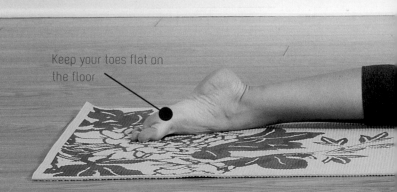

step 6 Lift your gaze slightly to bring your chin parallel to the floor. Hold for a few breaths.

step 7 Return to Downward Facing Dog. Repeat on the other side.

Keep your knee above your ankle.

45

TWISTED LOW-LUNGE POSE

Are you ready for a move with a twist? Twisting poses tighten up your core and the muscles of your back. If you have a yoga block and strap, keep them handy. You can use one or both props to modify this move.

Low-Lunge Pose

step 1   Start in Low-Lunge Pose with your right foot forward.

step 2   Put your left hand on the mat while you bring your right hand to the top of your right knee. Press into your right hand to turn your chest open to the right. Take a few deep breaths. If this feels challenging, stay here.

step 3   If you want more of a stretch, bend your left knee to bring your heel close to your bottom. Reach back with your right hand to take the outside of your left ankle.

step 4 Gently kick your left foot away from your bottom to engage the muscles in your left leg. Hold for a few breaths.

step 5 Return to Downward Facing Dog Pose. Repeat on the other side.

Downward Facing Dog

WIDE LOW-LUNGE POSE

The Wide Low-Lunge Pose provides a deep stretch for the hips, thighs, and lower back. It may not have a Sanskrit name, but with a stretch like that, it's quite a popular yoga pose.

step 1 Start in Downward Facing Dog Pose. Step your right foot to the outside of your right hand. Make sure your left toes point straight forward.

step 2 Keep your left knee lifted as you slowly lower your hips to bring your shoulders over your wrists. Keep your right knee hugging into your right shoulder. If this feels challenging, stay here for a few breaths.

step 2

If the stretch in the hip and buttock is too intense for you in this pose, bring your left knee down to the mat.

step 3 If you are interested in a more intense stretch, slowly lower to your forearms one at a time. Bring your elbows just under your shoulders on the mat. Keep your left leg as straight as possible. Keep your right knee close to your right shoulder. Hold for a few breaths.

step 4 Return to Downward Facing Dog Pose. Repeat on the other side.

TWISTED EXTENDED HAND-TO-TOE POSE

Sanskrit Name: *Utthita Hasta Padangusthasana*

Pronounced: ooh-TEE-tah HAH-sta pah-dahn-goo-STAS-ah-nah

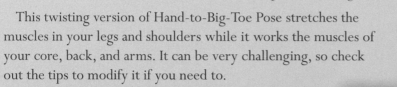

This twisting version of Hand-to-Big-Toe Pose stretches the muscles in your legs and shoulders while it works the muscles of your core, back, and arms. It can be very challenging, so check out the tips to modify it if you need to.

Mountain Pose

step 1   Start in Mountain Pose.

step 2   Lift your right foot off the ground by bringing the knee straight up into the air.

step 3   Take your left hand to the outside of the right foot. Rest your right hand on your right hip.

step 4   Stand tall by lifting your chin and straightening your back as much as you can. Slowly begin to straighten the right leg by pressing your foot forward. Your leg does not have to become completely straight, so stop straightening the knee when this stretch begins to feel intense.

step 5   Extend your right arm out behind you. Open your chest to the right.

step 6   Either look straight ahead or challenge yourself by looking back over your right thumb.

step 7   Hold for a few breaths. Return to Mountain Pose.

step 8   Repeat on the other side.

There are two easy ways to modify this pose:

1. If it's hard to reach your foot, try holding on to the outside of the knee instead. Do not extend the leg if you are holding the knee. Simply work on twisting open to the side instead.

2. If you can reach your foot but have difficulty straightening the leg, try wrapping a yoga strap around the foot to extend your reach. Then follow the rest of the directions for this pose.

BROKEN TOE POSE

You might think a lot about your shoes, but what about your feet? This pose stretches the tight muscles along the bottoms of your feet. It might feel intense, so start small. Try holding this pose for just a few breaths to start. Then work up to 30 seconds or even a minute.

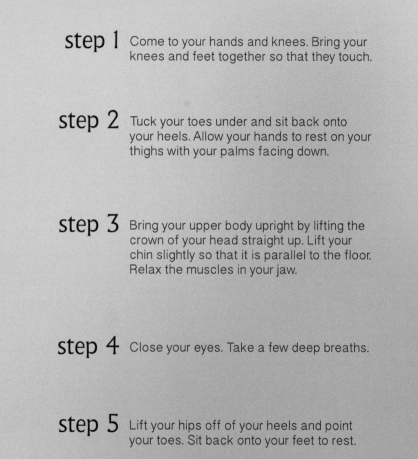

step 1 Come to your hands and knees. Bring your knees and feet together so that they touch.

step 2 Tuck your toes under and sit back onto your heels. Allow your hands to rest on your thighs with your palms facing down.

step 3 Bring your upper body upright by lifting the crown of your head straight up. Lift your chin slightly so that it is parallel to the floor. Relax the muscles in your jaw.

step 4 Close your eyes. Take a few deep breaths.

step 5 Lift your hips off of your heels and point your toes. Sit back onto your feet to rest.

This pose can feel very intense, but remember to stop what you're doing if you feel any pain.

Keep your back straight.

Tuck your toes under.

HERO POSE

Sanskrit Name: *Virasana*

Pronounced: veer-AHS-ah-nah

That's right, girl. Be a hero! Hero Pose stretches the muscles in the tops of the feet and thighs while also strengthening the low back. Because this pose allows you to sit fairly still, it can be a nice time to focus your thoughts on your breathing. When you begin working on this pose, you might only hold it for a few breaths. Over time, you may be able to sit in this pose for five minutes or more.

step 1 From your hands and knees, separate your feet so that they are slightly wider than your hips. Press the tops of your feet down into the mat.

step 2 Walk your hands back toward the outsides of your hips as you slowly sit between your heels.

step 3 Sit up tall by lifting the crown of your head straight up. Lift your chin slightly until it is parallel to the floor.

step 4 Draw your shoulder blades down. Pull your belly in.

step 5 Return to your hands and knees to rest.

If sitting between your ankles feels too intense or hurts your knees at all, try this modification: Place a block between your ankles and sit on it. You'll still get the great stretch and benefits of Hero Pose, but you won't hurt your knees.

Make Yoga WORK for You

A girl like you is probably swamped. You're busy with school, spending time with friends and family, and various other activities. It's exhausting! How can you add another activity to your already bursting schedule?

One of the best things about yoga is that you can customize it to fit your life. If you try a type of yoga that you don't enjoy, don't be discouraged. Try another type that sounds like a better match for you. Do you like your music quiet, loud, or extra loud? Do you crave serenity, or do you want to get pumped up during your workout? Different types of yoga go best with different atmospheres. Do a little research to find the perfect match for you.

Joining yoga classes is a great place to start, but that's not the only way to get a good yoga workout. If group exercise isn't your thing, try watching yoga classes online or following along with a yoga book. Many people enjoy freestyle home practices. This means that they simply do the poses that feel good to them for as long as they like. This unstructured type of yoga helps people recovering from injuries or those who just enjoy having creative freedom in their workouts.

You're the boss in your yoga class. Remember to listen to your body. If you feel sick or tired, take the day off or just do a less challenging workout. If you are injured, be extra careful about poses that work your injured body part.

Never be afraid to modify a pose. This might mean using a block or a strap to reach the floor or your feet. Or it might mean doing a pose slightly differently. After all, you may not be the best at yoga. Your goal should simply be to *feel* your best.

Namaste

Pronounced: NAH-mah-stay
Nama means "bow."
As means "I."
Te means "you."

Have you ever heard someone say "*Namaste?*" This Sanskrit word, usually spoken at the end of a yoga class, is a common greeting in India. The literal definition for this word is "I bow to you," or "I honor you." However, Namaste also has a deeper meaning. It is used to communicate that the speaker sees and honors the heart and spirit in another person. It is used to show deep respect for someone. Namaste is usually spoken with the hands held in front of the heart with the fingertips touching in a prayer-like position.

SET
Goals

From the Sanskrit vocabulary to the circus-performer poses, you might wonder if yoga is from a different planet. Yoga can be a little intimidating, but don't be afraid to give it a try. Start small by setting reasonable goals for yourself. You might decide to do one yoga workout a week. Or you could focus on trying to learn two new poses each week. Write your goals down somewhere you'll see often so you don't forget them.

Ask your friends if any of them are interested in learning about yoga. Having a "yoga buddy" is a great way to stay motivated. You can plan your yoga workouts together. You and your yoga buddy can help each other with body alignment and staying focused.

It doesn't take long to experience the benefits of yoga. Many people report feeling better after their very first practice. A regular yoga practice can help you become more fit, flexible, and happy. So what are you waiting for?

Glossary

alignment (uh-LYNE-muhnt)—the correct positioning of the body in order to reduce the chance of injury

core (KOHR)—the muscles of your stomach, chest, back and pelvis

meditation (med-uh-TAY-shuhn)—the practice of relaxing the mind and body by a regular program of mental exercise

modify (mah-duh-fih-KAY-shuhn)—to change a yoga pose in order to better suit a particular person's body

prop (PROP)—tool used to make different yoga poses easier

Sanskrit (SAN-skrit)—Ancient language from India written from left to right in a script called Devangari

READ MORE

Burns, Brian, Howard Kent, and Claire Hayler. *Yoga for Beginners.* From Couch to Conditioned: A Beginner's Guide to Getting Fit. New York: Rosen Pub., 2011.

Purperhart, Helen. *Yoga Exercises for Teens: Developing a Calmer Mind and a Stronger Body.* Alameda, Calif.: Hunter House Publishers, 2009.

Spilling, Michael. *Yoga Step-By-Step.* Skills in Motion. New York: Rosen Central, 2011.

Wood, Alix. *You Can Do Yoga.* Let's Get Moving! New York: Gareth Stevens Publishing, 2014.

INTERNET SITES

FactHound offers a safe, fun way to find Internet sites related to this book. All of the sites on FactHound have been researched by our staff.

Here's all you do:

Visit *www.facthound.com*

Type in this code: 9781491421208

ABOUT THE AUTHOR

Rebecca Rissman is a certified yoga instructor, nonfiction author, and editor. She has written books about history, culture, science, and art. Her book *Shapes in Sports* earned a starred review from *Booklist* magazine, and her series *Animal Spikes and Spines* received *Learning Magazine*'s 2013 Teachers Choice for Children's Books. She lives in Portland, Oregon, with her husband and daughter, and enjoys hiking, yoga, and cooking.

Index